Forces and Motion

Casey Rand

Raintree

Chicago, Illinois

© 2009 Raintree
an imprint of Capstone Global Library, LLC
Chicago, Illinois

Customer Service 888-454-2279
Visit our website at www.heinemannraintree.com

Editorial: Megan Cotugno, Andrew Farrow, and Clare Lewis
Design: Philippa Jenkins
Illustrations: KJA-artists.com
Picture Research: Ruth Blair
Production: Alison Parsons

Originated by Modern Age
Printed and bound in the United States of America, North Mankato MN

14 13 12
10 9 8 7 6 5 4 3 2

Library of Congress Cataloging-in-Publication Data
Rand, Casey.
 Forces and motion / Casey Rand. -- 1st ed.
  p. cm. -- (Sci-hi. Physical science)
 Includes bibliographical references and index.
 ISBN 978-1-4109-3249-5 (hc) -- ISBN 978-1-4109-3264-8 (pb) 1. Force and energy--Juvenile literature. 2. Motion--Juvenile literature. I. Title.
 QC73.4.R36 2008
 531'.6--dc22
                    2008026154

Acknowledgments
The author and publishers are grateful to the following for permission to reproduce copyright material: © Corbis/Darren Staples/Reuters p. **25**; © Corbis/David Katzenstein p. **31**; © Corbis/David Madison p. **27**; © Corbis/Duomo p. **41** (bottom); © Corbis/Jack Hollingsworth p. **9**; © Corbis/Ken Davies pp. **iii** (Contents, bottom), **30**; © Corbis/Michael S. Yamashita p. **39**; © Corbis/Oliver Furrer/Brand X p. **23**; © Corbis/moodboard p. **7**; © Corbis/Reuters pp. **37**, **41** (top); © Corbis/Stefanie Grewel/zefa p. **29**; © Corbis/Tim Tadder pp. **iii** (Contents, top), **14**, **16**; © Corbis/Transtock p. **32** (top); © Getty Images/AFP p. **10**; © Getty Images/News p. **32** (bottom); © Getty Images/The Image Bank p. **19**; © naturepl/David Cotteridge p. **21**; © naturepl.com/John Waters p. **22**; © Photolibrary Group pp. **13**, **15**, **35**; © Photolibrary Group/Bilderlounge p. **4**; © Photolibrary Group/workbookstock pp. **6**, **12**, **40**; © Science Photo Library p. **20**; © Science Photo Library/European Space Agency p. **8**; © Science Photo Library/NASA p. **28**; © Science Photo Library/Sheila Terry p. **34**; © Science Photo Library/Prof. Stewart Lowther p. **5**; © Shutterstock background images and design features throughout.

Cover photographs reproduced with permission of © Getty Images **main**; © Corbis/Mark A. Johnson **inset**.

The publishers would like to thank literacy consultant Nancy Harris and content consultant John Pucek for their assistance in the preparation of this book.

Some words are shown in bold, **like this**. These words are explained in the glossary. You will find important information and definitions underlined and in bold, **<u>like this</u>**.

072012
006804RP

Contents

What forces are acting on this swimmer?

Go to page 14 for the answer.

How much total momentum does this construction truck have?

Find out on page 30!

Throughout the book, you'll find abbreviations that reference distance and speed. See page 43 to find out what they mean.

FORCES AND MOTION

Motion is movement. Everything is moving and all movement begins with **force**.

All around us

Even when a person stands very still his or her heart continues to beat, pumping blood through their veins. The Earth moves around the Sun, and the whole solar system moves in space.

All movement is caused by force. Some forces are easy to see, such as the girl kicking the soccer ball in the photo below. Others, like the **magnetic field** used to lift a car in a scrapyard, are invisible but can be very powerful!

This girl uses her muscles to generate the force to kick the ball in the air.

What is physics?

Physics is the study of force and the movement it creates. What speeds can a skydiver reach falling to Earth? What forces do firefighters use to battle fires? How does a fighter jet take flight from an aircraft carrier? Physics can answer all of these questions and more!

VOLCANO POWER!

It is estimated that the volcanic eruption of Mount St. Helens in Washington state in 1980 generated as much force every second as an atomic bomb! The eruption lasted for 9 hours. In total, the eruption generated the same force as over 32,000 atomic bombs!

The strongest forces are those created by nature.

Defining Forces

Forces are all around us and within us. Our muscles must generate force for us to be able to walk, talk, or even just to breathe. Earth generates a force that holds us down so we don't float away.

What is a force?

A force is simply a push or pull. The chair you are sitting on or the floor you are standing on is being pushed down by your weight. But to hold you up, the chair or floor is pushing you back.

The force of water pushes the surfboard. It speeds the surfer towards the shore.

What do forces do?

When forces push or pull on an object, they can cause lots of action to happen. Forces can cause objects to fall, rise, turn, compress, stretch, speed up, or slow down. Not all forces cause an action to happen though. Some forces are too weak to cause any motion. Some forces are balanced out by forces acting on the same object.

How do forces happen?

Forces result from an interaction between two objects. For example, when a tennis racket hits a tennis ball, it pushes the ball away. The interaction between the racket and the ball resulted in force. As soon as the interaction between the racket and ball is over, the force is over as well. The tennis ball may continue to move quickly away, but the ball is no longer feeling the force of the racket.

The tennis ball and racket exchange forces only while they interact.

Can You Feel the Force?

All forces are described as either **contact forces** or **noncontact forces**. Touching objects that pull or push on one another are using contact forces. Some forces can push or pull one another from far away, without even touching! These forces are known as noncontact forces.

Noncontact forces

Let's start with these sometimes invisible forces! Noncontact forces surround us all the time, but they can be harder to see. When you try to pull a magnet from the fridge the magnet pulls itself back toward the fridge. The magnetic force is invisible but very real. An example of a noncontact force is **gravity**.

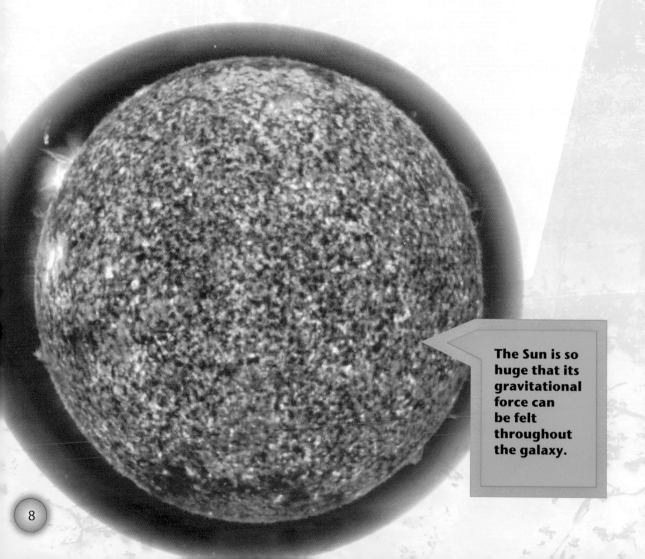

The Sun is so huge that its gravitational force can be felt throughout the galaxy.

Contact forces

Most contact forces are easy to see, for example, when someone throws a ball or pushes a cart. This force is known as **applied force**. It is simply the force a person or thing applies to another person or thing when they push or pull it.

A **spring force** is another type of contact force. This is the force a compressed or stretched spring puts on an object with which it is in contact. When a person jumps on a trampoline, it is spring force that causes him or her to bounce high!

The frisbee is thrown using a contact force known as applied force.

Balanced and Unbalanced Forces

Most of the time objects have many **forces** acting on them at once! <u>**If a force is pushing an object in one direction, and an equal force is pulling in the opposite direction, the forces are balanced.**</u> If a force is pushing or pulling on an object and is not balanced by other forces, it is said to be unbalanced. When an **unbalanced force** is acting on an object, the object will change its size, shape, or motion.

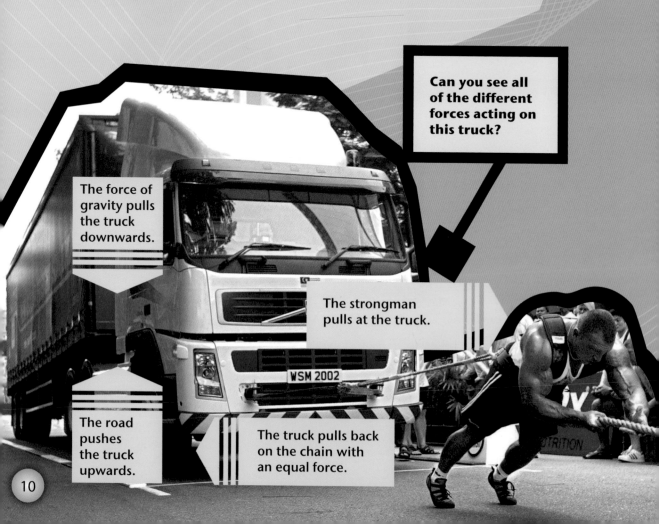

Can you see all of the different forces acting on this truck?

The force of gravity pulls the truck downwards.

The strongman pulls at the truck.

The road pushes the truck upwards.

The truck pulls back on the chain with an equal force.

WSM 2002

Equilibrium

When all forces acting on an object are balanced, the object is in **equilibrium**. When an object is in equilibrium, its motion will not change. If it is motionless, it will remain motionless. If it is moving, it will keep moving.

The strongman on the opposite page is trying to pull a truck, but it is not moving. The force of gravity is pulling the truck down, but the road pushes back up on the truck and holds it in place. The up and down forces on the truck are balanced. The strongman in the picture is using his strength to try to pull at the truck, but the truck is too heavy and pulls back on the chain with an equal force. This situation is equilibrium!

Tug-of-War

Sometimes, the forces acting on an object are equal and in opposite directions. In the first game of tug-of-war (below), the pull by the red team equals the pull by the blue team. The forces are balanced, and the rope is in equilibrium. It does not move.

However, when more force is added to the red side of the rope, like in the second game, the forces no longer cancel each other out. Now, the pull by the red team is stronger than the pull by the blue team. The forces are unbalanced. The red team wins the game!

Which game is an example of equilibrium? The top or bottom?

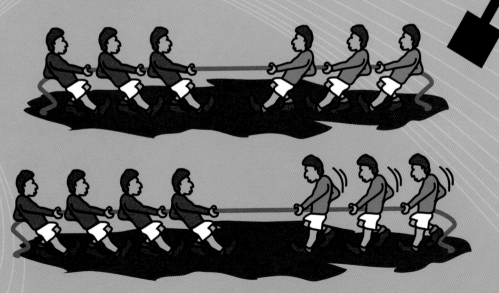

SIMPLE MACHINES AT WORK

Everyday we use tools called **simple machines** to magnify the **forces** we produce. Imagine trying to open a can of beans with your bare hands! You could use a can opener, a simple machine based on the **lever** and **inclined plane**, to magnify your force and make this job much easier.

Simple machines in firefighting

There are six different types of simple machines. Let's look at how firefighters use five of these to fight fires and rescue people.

The inclined plane formed by the ladder makes climbing to the rescue much easier.

The wheel:

Firefighters use huge vehicles designed to speedily move them and their equipment to the fire. Their fire engines use the wheel to reduce the amount of force required to move the heavy truck. Imagine trying to move a car or truck without wheels!

The wedge and the lever:

Firefighters use an axe made up of two simple machines. The sharp end of the axe is a wedge that can be used to chop holes and cut wood. The opposite end of the axe is similar to the claw end of a hammer, which allows the axe to be used as a lever to pry doors and windows open.

The inclined plane:

The ladder on a fire truck can extend at an angle to reach a window or rooftop. This forms a ramp, or an inclined plane, which makes it easier for the firefighters to climb up to the windows of a burning building and rescue victims.

The screw:

A fire hydrant is like a plug that holds back a tremendous amount of water. Fire hydrants rely on a simple machine known as a screw. When a fire occurs, a fire fighter can release the screw and gain access to the water.

Firefighters use an axe to chop holes into rooftops and walls and to pry down doors and windows.

The pulley:

The last simple machine is a **pulley**. While it is not often used by firefighters, a pulley is used to raise a flag. A person stands at the bottom of a flagpole and pulls on a rope. The pulley allows the flag to move high up the flagpole.

FRICTION

Friction is a force that works against motion. If you push very gently on your textbook as it rests on the table it will resist a certain amount of your force before starting to slide across the table. This resistance is friction.

Friction: the enemy of motion

<u>Friction is a force caused when two surfaces are in contact with each other</u>. It prevents the two objects sliding past each other. Friction can be seen between two solid objects, like when you rub your hands together. It can be seen between a solid and a liquid, like when you try to swim through water. It can even be seen between a solid and a gas, like when you throw a ball and air slows it down.

Even liquids like water apply frictional forces to oppose motion.

Water, in the form of snow, can also act as a lubricant.

Where does friction come from?

Even objects that appear very smooth are covered in tiny bumps and holes that snag together when they are in contact with other surfaces. This snagging causes friction.

Two types of friction

If you attempted to slide a heavy box across the floor you would experience two types of friction. Getting the box to start sliding would be much more difficult than keeping the box sliding once it is moving. **Starting friction**, or static friction, is much stronger than **sliding friction**.

Overcoming friction

In many situations, it is necessary to reduce friction, for example, to keep the parts of a car engine moving smoothly. A common method is to use **lubricants**. A lubricant is any substance that reduces the effects of friction, such as oil or water.

Friction: the friend of motion?

It may seem that friction is the enemy of motion. It slows us down when we are running or cycling. However, just imagine trying to walk or drive without friction. It would be worse than trying to walk or drive on ice! Think about the three examples on the next page.

This cyclist uses friction to slow down her bike and break when necessary.

Friction for grip

Imagine the handle of a hammer, golf club, or softball bat. The ends or handles are often covered in a rough material to create friction, which makes gripping them easier.

Friction for turning

Tires and sneakers are made with rubber that has extra bumps and holes created in their surfaces to increase friction. This is known as tread or traction. Without the friction created by the tread, a bicycle would be nearly impossible to turn.

Friction for braking

The brakes on a bike are made of special pads. These grip the tire when the brakes are squeezed. The pads create friction to slow the wheels and bike down.

Do You Know?

As the bicycle speeds down the road, frictional forces are acting against the motion of the bike trying to slow it down. Is the frictional force acting in this situation starting friction or sliding friction?

Answer on page 43.

RISING AND FALLING FORCES

Why does a massive submarine float in water while a small rock sinks quickly? Why does a skydiver fall so quickly and what **force** does a parachute use to slow the fall? This chapter examines the forces of rising and falling.

Buoyancy

Have you ever tried to push a football underwater? If you have, you know that the water pushes the ball back toward you. This force is called **buoyancy**. It is the upward force that any liquid or gas puts on an object that is floating in it.

Buoyancy is equal to the weight of the gas or liquid an object pushes out of the way. An object will sink in a liquid until it pushes away enough of the liquid to produce enough buoyancy to hold up its weight.

Sink or float?

Submarines are made with special chambers that can be filled or emptied of water. A submarine is huge and pushes a lot of the water out of the way. When the chambers are empty, the submarine is light enough that the buoyancy of the water pushes it up and it floats. When the chambers are filled, however, the submarine is too heavy and it sinks below the surface of the water.

Special chambers allow the submarine to change its weight depending on whether it wants to sink or float.

What goes up, must come down

Any object thrown or launched away from the surface of Earth will feel an attraction to come back down to the surface of the earth. This attraction is **gravity**. It affects everything.

Gravity is a downward attractive force that exists between Earth and all objects near it. Near the surface of Earth, gravity causes all objects to **accelerate** or pick up speed as they fall.

Everything feels gravity

All objects feel the attractive forces of gravity. All objects, no matter how big or small, experience the same acceleration due to gravity. On the Moon, where there is no air and no air resistance, a feather will fall as fast as a bowling ball!

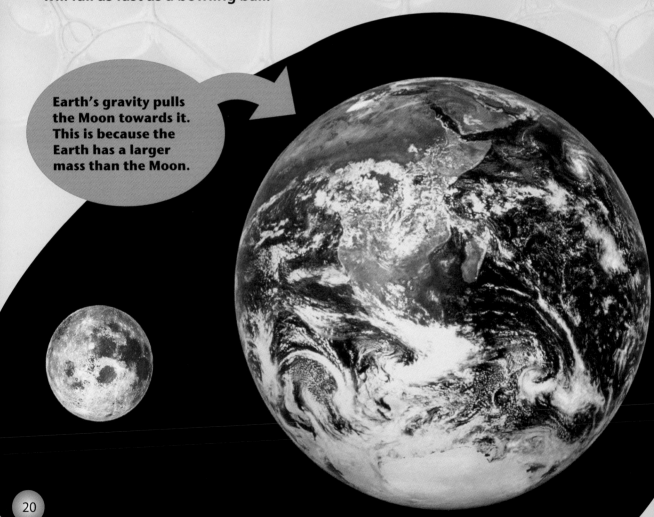

Earth's gravity pulls the Moon towards it. This is because the Earth has a larger mass than the Moon.

Everything has gravity

All objects feel the attractive forces of gravity. Look back at the photo on page 20. The Earth's gravitational force pulls at the Moon. And you possess some gravitational force, too! The amount of this force that each object has depends on its **mass**, or how much stuff it is made of. A larger mass means an object has more gravitational attraction. Gravity is a weak force so it takes a very large mass, like that of planets and moons, to have enough gravity to be felt.

The scientist Galileo was the first scientist to show that gravity accelerates all objects at the same rate. He may have demonstrated this by dropping balls of different mass off the Leaning Tower of Pisa at the same time to show that they would land at the same time.

The Leaning Tower of Pisa

Falling from the sky

How can you reach speeds faster than the fastest roller coaster without the roller coaster or any other machine? Skydiving is the answer! Skydivers use the force of gravity to reach great speeds falling toward the earth.

Gravity vs. air resistance

As a skydiver falls downward due to gravity, air pushes upward against the skydiver. This is a special type of friction known as **air resistance**. Gravity pulls down to speed the skydiver up while air resistance pushes up to slow the skydiver down.

Terminal velocity

The top speed that a skydiver will reach while falling is known as **terminal velocity**. As the skydiver falls faster and faster, air pushes back harder and harder. Eventually, the upward force of the air equals the downward force of gravity. At this point, the object continues to fall at its current velocity or speed but no longer speeds up. When a skydiver reaches terminal velocity, her or she is in **equilibrium**.

The peregrine falcon is the speed king of the air. Its streamlined body helps it to travel at extraordinary speeds.

Terminal velocity is 200 kilometers per hour (124 miles per hour) in a free fall. Terminal velocity increases to nearly 322 kph (200 mph) when the skydiver balls up. When the parachute is released, terminal velocity falls to a safe landing speed of only 24 kph (15 mph) in less than 5 seconds!

A skydiver can fall faster by straightening out and diving head first toward the ground. This is known as streamlining.

Terminal velocity for the average skydiver is about 200 kph (124 mph). However, at this speed the skydiver still could not catch up to a peregrine falcon diving for its prey. The top speed of the peregrine falcon is almost 322 kph (200 mph). To keep up with the falcon the skydiver would have to pull all of his limbs in to his body and curl up into a ball. Then, the skydiver could keep up with our speedy flying friend. Well, almost!

Mass and Weight

The average rugby player weighs nearly 100 kg (220 lb). Did you know, however, that if you put the average big, strong rugby player on the Moon, he would weigh just over 16 kg (35 lb)? **Mass** and **weight** are often thought of as the same thing, but they are actually very different.

Weight

The force of the downward pull of gravity on an object is known as weight. When a person stands on a bathroom scale, the scale tells him his weight. On the Moon where gravity is not as strong as it is on Earth, the weight of a rugby player, or any object, is much less than it is on Earth. Similarly, on a massive planet such as Jupiter, the weight of the rugby player would be much greater than it is on Earth. In deep outer space, far away from any planets, the weight of a rugby player would be 0 kg.

Mass

The amount of matter something contains, or how much stuff it is made up of, is measured by mass. Mass cannot be measured on a scale that relies on gravity, it is measured on a balance that compares an unknown mass to a known mass. On the Moon or in deep outer space, the mass of an object that is 1 kg on earth will still be 1 kg. Mass does not rely on gravity.

Weight vs. Mass

	WEIGHT	MASS
It measures	pull of gravity on object	matter contained in object
The instrument used to measure it	scale	balance
What happens in deep space (no gravity)?	does not exist	same as on Earth

If these rugby players were on the Moon, their weights would change. Their masses would not.

Speed and Velocity

Earth travels millions of miles around the sun each year at speeds of 105,000 kph (65,000 mph). The average **velocity** of the Earth after its one year orbit is complete is 0 kph! **Speed** and velocity are often confused as the same thing, but they are actually very different. To understand the differences between speed and velocity, we must first understand **distance** and **displacement**. These are the measurements that speed and velocity are based on.

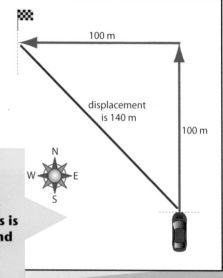

100 m

displacement is 140 m

100 m

N
W   E
S

The distance the car travels is different than the displacement. This is why final speed and velocity of the car are not the same.

Distance and displacement

If the car in the diagram above traveled around along the blue arrows shown above, the total distance traveled by the car would be 200 meters. The car traveled 100 meters north and 100 meters east. **Distance simply measures the total length traveled.**

Displacement considers both distance and direction. It always equals the shortest distance between the starting and finishing points. The total displacement of the car after traveling along the blue arrows is represented by the red line that leads from an object's starting point to the object's finishing point. So although the car traveled 200 meters, its final displacement is only about 140 meters northwest.

Measurement name	What it measures
Distance	Total distance traveled from point A to point B (XX m)
Displacement	Shortest possible distance from point A to point B (XX m)

Speed and velocity

Speed = Distance/Time   *Velocity = Displacement/Time*

Speed is simply a measure of how fast you are going. The direction you are going does not matter. **Velocity is a measure of how fast you are going in a certain direction.** When the car on page 26 traveled north along the first blue arrow it had a velocity of about 65 kph (40 mph) north. When the car turned west, its velocity north dropped to 0 kph (0 mph).

> **What is the average velocity of this race car at the end of a race? Find out below!**

Did you know?

Formula 1 (F1) race cars reach great speeds and velocities during races. The average speed of most F1 racers is over 300 kph (186 mph) at the end of a race. Did you know, however, that the average velocity of the same racers, at the end of the same race, is 0 kph! This is because the race car starts and finishes in the same place, so the total displacement of the car at the end of the race is 0 meters.

ACCELERATION

To leave the **atmosphere**, space shuttles must reach speeds of over 29,000 kph (18,000 mph). How do these shuttles go from sitting on the launch pad to blasting through the sky at super fast speeds? **Acceleration** is the answer!

What is acceleration?

<u>**All changes in velocity, both increases and decreases, are known as acceleration.**</u> Acceleration is the rate at which an object changes its velocity.

velocity/time = acceleration

Forces and acceleration

In order for an object to accelerate (to speed up or slow down), a force must be applied to the object. The velocity of an object can change as time goes on. For instance, a bike rider can use the force of his or her muscles to pedal harder and increase velocity. This is a positive acceleration of the bicycle. The bike rider can also squeeze the brakes, which increases frictional forces and decreases velocity. This is a negative acceleration of the bicycle.

The powerful engines push the shuttle to great accelerations.

Speeding up

As a biker begins to pedal, the bike's velocity will increase by a certain amount as it accelerates.

Slowing down

When the velocity of an object is decreasing, it has a negative value for acceleration. As the biker squeezes the brakes, the bike will slow down. The velocity will decrease over a certain amount of time.

The biker can accelerate by applying a force to the pedals or by squeezing the brakes.

Momentum

Momentum is a measurement of how much force it would take to stop an object's motion.

Mass in motion

All objects have **mass**, so any object that has motion also has momentum. The amount of momentum any object has depends both on the object's mass and on the **velocity** of its motion.

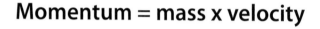

Momentum = mass x velocity

This formula tells us that momentum will increase if either the mass or velocity of an object increases.

A massive truck picks up lots of momentum even at slow speeds.

A remote control truck cannot gain the same momentum as a real truck, even with great speeds.

Massive momentum

The small remote control truck in the above picture has a mass of 5 kg. When it reaches its top **speed** of 15 m/s it has a total momentum of:

Momentum = mass x velocity = 5 kg x 15 m/s = 75 kg x m/s

The huge truck on the opposite page has a mass of 10,000 kg. It has a much larger mass than the remote control truck. If it is moving at only 1 m/s which truck will have a greater momentum? Remember momentum is equally dependent on both velocity and mass! If the construction truck has a mass of 10,000 kg its total momentum is:

Momentum = mass x velocity= 10,000 kg x 1 m/s = 10,000 kg x m/s

So even though the velocity of the remote control truck is much larger, its momentum is much smaller. We can now see that the slow moving construction truck would be much harder to stop than a fast moving remote control truck.

Off-Road Racing

The Dodge Tomahawk is considered by many to be the fastest motorcycle in the world. It has a reported top speed of over 600 kph (375 mph) and can **accelerate** from 0 to 100 kph (62 mph) in just over 2.5 seconds.

Trophy trucks are some of the fastest off-road vehicles in the world. These trucks can reach speeds of 200 kph (125 mph) even in rough terrain. They are built tough to withstand bumps, hills, mud, rocks, and other obstacles.

What would happen if these two fast vehicles raced? Let's find out!

Trophy truck

Tomahawk motorcycle

The race course

Suppose the Tomahawk and a trophy truck were planning to race from the top of the hill (point A) to the bottom of the hill (point B). The **distance** from point A to point B along the road is 300 km (187 miles). The **displacement**, or shortest possible distance, from point A to point B is 100 km (62 miles). However this route is mostly rocky, muddy trails that the Tomahawk can't travel along, so it will have to take the road. The trophy truck, however, can travel directly from point A to point B along the rocky, muddy trails.

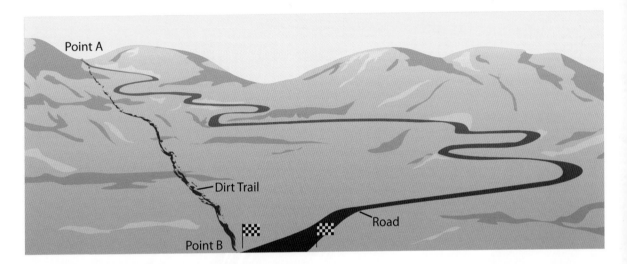

Point A

Dirt Trail

Road

Point B

Who will win?

If the average speed for the entire race of the Tomahawk is 480 kph (300 mph) as it travels along the road and the trophy truck has an average speed of 160 kph (100 mph) as it travels along the dirt trail, who will cross the finish line at point B first?

Brainteasers!

1. When the Tomahawk travels from point A to point B along the road, it must travel a much greater distance than the trophy truck will travel to cross the finish line. How will the final displacement of each compare?

2. If the trophy truck reaches the finish line in 30 minutes, the average speed of the truck was 200 kph (125 mph). What was the average velocity (remember the truck's distance and displacement are equal)?

Answers on page 43.

NEWTON'S LAWS OF FORCE AND MOTION

The rest of this book will explore three laws developed by Sir Isaac Newton that changed the way scientists understand the universe. These laws explain how forces change the motion of objects.

Newton defined the laws of motion and laid the groundwork for much of modern science. His laws are still in use today.

Newton's first law of motion

Newton's first law has two parts:

1. **"An object that is not moving will not start moving unless acted upon by an unbalanced force."**
   This part is easy to see. If you don't pick up a bowling ball and roll it down the lane, it will not get up and roll down the lane on its own. The ball is not moving and it will need an unbalanced force (you) to get it moving.

2. **"An object that is moving will keep moving with the same speed and in the same direction unless acted upon by an unbalanced force."**
   This part of the law says that a force is not needed to keep an object that is in motion moving. Once something starts in motion, it will stay in motion unless it is forced to stop.

You know that if you pick up the bowling ball and roll it down the lane, it will be stopped by the pins and the wall at the end of the gutter. But if the lane was extended and the pins were 80 km (50 miles) away, your ball would never make it to the pins at the end. It would stop rolling long before this. Why? Newton's law tells us it that the ball comes to a stop because of the presence of force. There must be another force acting to slow down your ball. That force is friction. It is the unbalanced force that Newton said must act to change the motion of your ball. If you were to remove friction, it wouldn't matter how long the lane was. Your ball would keep rolling all the way to the pins!

The force of friction acts against the velocity of the bowling ball.

Newton's second law of Motion

We know forces cause an object to speed up or slow down. Newton's second law tells us exactly how much a force will cause an object to speed up or slow down. The law states that the relationship between an object's **mass** (m), **acceleration** (a), and the force (F) applied to the object is given by the formula:

Force = mass x acceleration or F=ma

This law tells us that a light object is much easier to push away or pull than a heavy object. If you push an empty shopping cart with all your force, it may speed away (accelerate) from you quite quickly. If you gave the same shopping cart, but this time filled with bricks, the same push, it would not speed away so quickly.

Force is measured in Newtons (N).
One Newton (N) = 1 kg x m/s^2

The world's most massive plane

One of the world's most massive planes is the Antonov An-225 (see the photo on the next page). It has a maximum takeoff mass of over 600,000 kg (1.3 million lb) or about the same mass as 300 average cars!

As the An-225 is accelerating for takeoff, the force of the engines is pushing the plane down the runway while the forces of friction and **air resistance** are pushing against the plane in the opposite direction.

Find the acceleration!

To find the acceleration of the plane, the **net force** on the plane must first be calculated as follows:

The force of the engines is 62 million N in the forward direction, and the force of friction and air resistance are a combined 2 million N in the backward direction. So, the net force is 60 million N in the forward direction. By using Newton's second law, we can work out the acceleration.

- We need to rearrange $F = ma$ to solve for acceleration: $a = F/m$

- Then plug in the numbers we already know so: $a = 60,000,000\ N/600,000\ kg$

- And solve: $a = 100\ m/s^2$

The massive An-225 will accelerate at $100\ m/s^2$ down the runway!

The massive An-225 requires a huge force to accelerate it down the runway.

Newton's third law of motion

Newton' third law states that for every action there is an equal and opposite reaction. All forces happen in pairs. The pair of forces are known as the action and reaction forces. When object A pushes (the action force) on object B, there is always an equal and opposite push (the reaction force) exerted by object B back on object A.

If you push against a wall, the wall will push you back. In fact, it will push you back with the same force you use to push it. The harder you push the wall, the harder it will push you. It is easier to see if you sit on a chair with wheels and push against the wall. Now the wall pushes you away. If you push the wall harder it will push you away even faster and further.

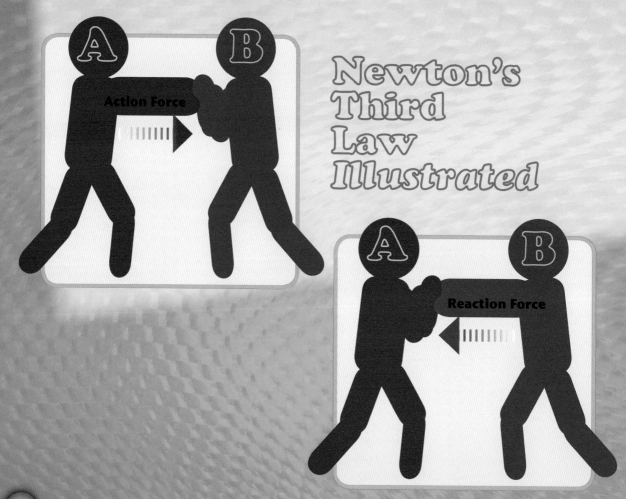

Newton's
Third
Law
Illustrated

Sumo wrestling

Two giant men each weighing over 200 kg (440 lb) enter a small ring. They each prepare to push each other out of the ring.

According to Newton's third law, when the first wrestler pushes against the second wrestler (action force) then the second wrestler must push back with an equal force (reaction force). Even though the wrestlers are putting equal forces on each other, one wrestler will still push the other out of the ring. Although the force of the action and reaction are always equal, they don't always produce the same result. The wrestler with the greater momentum (remember **momentum = mass x velocity**) will force the other wrestler to accelerate backward and out of the ring.

The action and reaction forces are equal and opposite.

Ironman and Newton's laws

The Ironman Triathlon is an annual race that includes a 3.9 km (2.4 mile) swim, a 180 km (112 mile) bike ride, and a 42.195 km (26.2 mile) run. Let's see how the laws of force and motion we have learned about apply to the race!

Action and reaction in the water

The first stretch of the Ironman race is the swim. As the racer swims through the water, we can see Newton's third law in action. The competitor in the picture uses his arms and legs to push the water backward (the **action force**). Since all actions happen in pairs, we know that the water will in turn push the swimmer forward (the **reaction force**).

The Ironman racer uses the water to propel forward.

Overcoming frictional forces

After the swim, the competitors move quickly to their bikes where they immediately start their ride. The racer begins to push the pedals harder and harder. He is applying Newton's second law, to accelerate the bicycle as quickly as possible. The bicycle is a very efficient instrument. Once the bicycle reaches a fast **velocity** and is on a flat surface, the racer can take advantage of Newton's first law.

The racer might give his legs some rest. The bicycle will keep moving at a nearly constant speed, without requiring the rider to add more force. However, frictional forces, both from the ground and the air, will eventually slow the bicycle down. The racers wear streamlined helmets to reduce these effects as much as possible.

The racer overcomes frictional forces on the bike.

Race to the finish

The final stretch of the Ironman race is a full marathon! The competitors use the tired muscles in their legs to generate as much force as possible to push them along to the finish.

And, it's a push of force to the finish!

Forces and Motion Review

Force

Forces are all around us. Remember that a force can be any push or pull. **Noncontact forces** are those where two objects not in contact with each other are pushing or pulling one another. **Gravity** is a special type of noncontact force that all objects have. **Weight** is a measurement of the pull of gravity on an object, while **mass** does not depend on gravity.

Motion

Remember that **velocity = displacement/time**, and displacement must consider direction. So, a racer can have great average speeds while still having no average velocity. To reach great velocities an object must first **accelerate**. **Remember that acceleration = change in velocity/change in time.**

Momentum is a measurement of the amount of force it would take to stop an object's motion. It is calculated using **momentum = mass x velocity.**

Newton's laws of force and motion

Sir Isaac Newton developed three laws dealing with force and motion. The first law told us the motion of an object will not change without the addition of an **unbalanced force**. Newton's second law gave us this equation: **F = mass x acceleration**, which tells us that lighter objects are easier to accelerate. The third law said that for every action there is an equal but opposite reaction.

Abbreviation Key

kilometer = km (miles = mi)
kilometers per hour = kph (miles per hour = mph)
kilogram = kg (pounds = lb)
meter = m (feet = ft)
meters per second = m/s
meters per second squared = m/s^2
Newton=N

Answer Key!

FROM PAGE 17: Sliding friction

FROM PAGE 33:
For the Tomahawk: 300 km\480 kph = 37.5 minutes
For the Trophy truck: 100 km\160 kph = 37.5 minutes
Answer: It's a tie!
Question 1. The displacement will be equal for the truck and Tomahawk, because the both start and finish at the same point.
Question 2. The average velocity is equal to the average speed of 200 kph. The truck's distance and displacement are equal.

Glossary

Acceleration The rate of change of velocity with respect to time

Air resistance Force that air exerts on a moving body

Applied force A type of contact force. It is the force that a person or thing applies or puts on another person or thing when it is pushed or pulled.

Atmosphere All of the gases that surround an object, such as a planet, in outer space

Balanced forces Two or more forces, applied to an object at the same time, that are equal in strength, so that no motion occurs

Buoyancy The upward force exerted on an object by a fluid

Contact force Force between two objects that are in physical contact with each other

Displacement The shortest possible difference between the initial position of something and its final position

Distance How far something traveled without respect to direction

Equilibrium The state an object is in when all forces acting on it are balanced

Force A push or pull

Free fall Fall of an object that is being acted on only by gravity

Friction The force that resists motion between two bodies in contact

Gravity The downward force that an object feels toward the surface of the earth or other planets

Inclined plane A plane surface used as a simple machine used to raise or lower a load

Inertia A property of matter by which it remains at rest or in uniform motion in the same straight line unless acted upon by some external force

Lever A device consisting of a bar that can be turned around a fixed point. You can use it to change the place at which you exert a force, the direction of the force, and the strength of the force.

Lubricant Any substance capable of reducing friction between two objects, such as oil or water

Magnetic field The area in which a magnet's pull has an effect

Mass Measure of how much matter or "stuff" an object contains

Momentum A measurement of how much force it would take to stop an objects motion. It is equal to the product of the body's mass and velocity.

Net force The sum of forces acting on an object

Newton Basic unit of force

Noncontact force Force between two objects that are not in physical contact with each other

Physics The study of force and the movement it creates

Pulley Simple machine made of linked wheels that increases the force a person can exert

Simple machines Tools that use the laws of physics to make work easier

Sliding friction The force that resists motion between two bodies in contact once the bodies are in motion

Speed The rate of change of distance of an object with respect to time

Spring force A type of contact force. It is the force of a compressed or stretched object.

Starting friction The force that resists motion between two bodies in contact when the bodies are not yet in motion. It is also called static friction.

Terminal velocity The velocity at which the downward force of gravity acting on an object equals the upward force of air resistance

Unbalanced forces Two or more forces acting on an object at the same time that are unequal in strength, so that one force overcomes the other (or others) and produces motion in its direction

Velocity The rate of change of displacement of an object with respect to time

Weight Measure of the gravitational pull on an object

Further Information

Books to read

Angliss, Sarah, and Maggie Hewson. *Forces and Motion*. New York: Kingfisher, 2001.

DiSpezio, Michael A. *Awesome Experiments in Forces and Motion.* New York: Sterling, 2006.

Gardner, Robert. *Forces and Motion Science Fair Projects Using Water Balloons, Pulleys, and Other Stuff*. Berkeley Heights, NJ: Enslow Publishers, 2004.

Gleason, Katherine. *Awesome Science*. Danbury, CT: Children's Press, 2004.

Goodstein, Madeline. *Science Fair Success Using Newton's Laws of Motion*. Berkeley Heights, NJ: Enslow Publishers, 2002.

Halls, Kelly Millner. *Science Fair Projects: Forces and Motion*. Chicago: Heinemann Library, 2008.

Hopwood, James. *Cool Gravity Activities.* Minneapolis, MN: Abdo, 2008.

Juettner, Bonnie. *Motion*. Chicago: Kidhaven Press, 2004.

Kravetz, Jonathan. *Graphic Organizers in Science: Forces and Motion*. Rosen, 2007.

Lafferty, Peter. *Eyewitness: Forces and Motion*. New York: DK, 1999.

Mason, Paul. *The Extreme Zone: Forces and Motion*. Chicago: Raintree, 2006.

Parker, Barry. *The Mystery of Gravity*. Tarrytown, NY: Marshall Cavendish, 2003.

Salas, Laura Purdie. *Discovering Nature's Laws: A Story About Isaac Newton*. Minneapolis, MN: Lerner Publishing, 2004.

Smith, Alastair, and others. *Energy, Forces and Motion*. New York: Scholastic, 2001.

Snedden, Robert. *Forces and Motion*. Strongsville, OH: Gareth Stevens, 2007.

Williams, Zella. *Experiments with Physical Science*. New York: Rosen Publishing, 2007.

Websites

http://www.school.discoveryeducation.com/
A website with lots of great activities that you can do at home that are geared toward science learning.

http://www.exploratorium.edu/ronh/weight
Find your weight on other planets! This site also helps you understand the differences between mass and weight. Fun and fascinating!

http://www.learner.org/interactives/parkphysics/coaster/
An interactive site that deals with amusement park physics. Design your own roller coaster!

http://www.harcourtschool.com/activity/newton/index.html
An interactive site that makes the relationship of force, mass, and acceleration both understandable and fun!

http://www.learningscience.org/psc2bmotionforces.htm
There are loads of interactive games and activities at this site. Covers forces and motion, physics, and more!

http://www.engineeringinteract.org/
Think you can beat an engineer in science! Quiz yourself at this engaging and colorful site!

Look It Up!

Do some more research on one or more of these topics:
• Newton's Laws of Force and Motion
• Terminal velocity and the peregrine falcon
• Dodge Tomahawk
• Ironman Triathlon (Maybe one day you will want to compete!)

Index